BEYOND MY MOMENT OF TRUTH

BEYOND MY MOMENT OF TRUTH

DAVID T. GILBERT.

Order this book online at www.trafford.com
or email orders@trafford.com

Most Trafford titles are also available at major online book retailers.

Printed in the United States of America.

ISBN: 978-1-4669-1290-8 (sc)
ISBN: 978-1-4669-1289-2 (e)

Trafford rev. 01/27/2012

 www.trafford.com

North America & international
toll-free: 1 888 232 4444 (USA & Canada)
phone: 250 383 6864 ♦ fax: 812 355 4082

CONTENTS

AUTHOR'S NOTE

PLEASE TAKE NOTE that those poems contained within this book that express a point of view, or an opinion about life principles, should not be regarded as 'absolute truth', but should be interpreted as by the above, as a point of view or an opinion only.

I have been with the Lord now for the best part of 32 years, and what I have written about was due to what I have observed within a Church situation, or because of observance through the eyes of a Spirit filled, born again believer.

All of the work that I do is actually based on fact, or factual events, and is due to having preference to writing about those things that occurred in my life that are based on truth, or have been experienced by me first hand.

I believe very strongly that when the task that one puts one's hand to is based on fact and truth, then that work becomes an expression of the individuals character, and therefore comes with all the heart felt emotion that the individual has.

As for my opinion, or point of view on the work in question, these expressions are how I interpreted the situations and circumstances that I went through at that particular time, what I was thinking, and what I was going through emotionally, and spiritually. Everyone is entitled to an opinion, and all should be permitted to express that opinion in a peace-ful, non violent way, without duress.

I have chosen to express my opinion through my poetry, in order to stir up peaceful, open debate, and therefore open up opportunities for salvation, and maybe bring people into an awareness that, we serve a God who has no wish, or desire, to see anyone go to a lost eternity.

God has given us a choice, in which He will not interfere with, but regardless of our final decision, He will respect that decision, and grant your desire, so choose wisely. God bless your choosing, regardless,

David T. Gilbert.

INTRODUCTION

I LOVE THE challenge of poetry writing, because I find it causes one to use the imagination and the creative gift within, the proof of the success or failure of what is written can be measured by the reaction of people who are looking for good, well written and captivating work. My interest in poetry was aroused when I was just entering High School, but due to varying social pressures at the time, I did not pursue it in a serious way, and so I lost interest.

Please allow me to introduce myself; my name is David T. Gilbert, I am 58 years old, married with three adult children, two of which are wed, and am currently living in Gawler, South Australia, which is the southern gateway to the world reknown Barossa Valley.

I am a writer of 'Poetry Short Stories', and have already had my first book published, which is being used as a training tool for first time authors. This is due to the work I did on writing the back cover 'Author's Note', which was quite an achievement for a first time author. My style of poetry is easy to read and follow, and I enjoy leaving the reader in deep thought about the topic written. I have always wanted to tell my life story, but I didn't have many chances or options, until I was challenged by God to write my story under His instruction, and so I did.

Many tears were shed, sins forgiven, lessons learned, mistakes corrected, apologies accepted, attitudes dealt with, and so on, until the past was finally laid to rest. My only regret was for a girl I once knew, but hurt very badly, not by physical violence, but by emotional misappropriation, for want of a better word. But the past is sometimes better left alone, because some find it much harder to deal with the past than others.

There are more poetry items in this book than in my first, each having it's own intro, and each one different from the others. To me, intro's are important in telling the story or point I want to get across, in such a way that there are no upsets or offences to come to the surface, and each poem presents a different challenge to the reader, leaving the reader thinking and pondering the challenge presented.

My main focus is to reach out to all those people that feel as though life has given up on them, and they have nothing left to hope for, since their view of God is that they don't quite fit the criteria for Church attendance. They see themselves as un- worthy and hopeless in a world that only accepts and seeks after the perfect (in their view.), and rejects the imperfect, leaving them on the scrap heap. There are a couple of poems contained within this second book, dealing specifically with the subject of how people view Jesus and His followers before and after salvation, and the surprise most people get when they find that salvation is, according to God's Word, available to all who dare to take that step of faith, and believe God for who He is, and what He is able to do with a soul totally sold out to Him. Also, they find that the difference between Godly love and worldly love is like trying to mix a ton of bananas with School chalk, expecting to manufacture rocket fuel.

I, myself have lived a very fortunate life, and am blessed in many ways, and have much to thank my God for, especially His patience, mercy and tolerance, but mostly, for not giving up on me at a time when I needed Him most; His grace is truly amaizing, and I am forever in His debt.

I pray, above all else, that you have a different opinion of God after you read the contents of this book, and somehow find the boldness and good sense to humbly come before Him, giving Him due praise and honor,

God bless you all,
David T. Gilbert.

PREFACE TO 'BEYOND MY MOMENT OF TRUTH'

This is now my second book, and this compilation of poetry, as with my first book, was written with the assistance and guidance of God's Holy Spirit. As I was putting the first book together, My Moment Of Truth, I took note of any and every step I made in gathering all the bits and pieces together, and all the mistakes and time-consuming chores, and then I sat down to improve on the way I did things. So this book is quite an upgrade from the first, and it contains more poetry, but despite the above, both books were designed to complete my whole life story.

My first book was a miracle in itself, for a number of reasons; not only did it tell an actual biography, it was done entirely in poetry, and as a first time author, knowing nothing at all about 'self-publishing', my book made it onto the 'best seller's list of the Christian Post. There was also the Author's Note on the back cover, which inspired other first time authors on how to complete that section of their book.

Since first attempting to publish, I have learned a great deal about being an author, especially when it comes to making sure that all the bits come together in the right order. I have written about a variety of issues, mostly to do with how we see life, and it's associated challenges, and the more poetry I write, the better I get. But at the end of the day, I must give all the glory to my Lord, for without Him, I can do nothing (John 15:5).

My prayer for this book, as always, is that it encourages people to stop and think about how we present the Gospel to people, and realize that our objective is not to make ourselves comfortable and cozy on this dying planet, but to tell the world that Jesus is their only hope of salvation, regardless of race, color or gender, or what our feelings are toward them. Life is too short to waste it on futile, worldly activities, we need to prepare for heaven, NOW, before it is too late.

I trust you will be blessed as you read,

Yours in CHRIST JESUS,
David T. Gilbert.

INTRODUCTION TO 'FUTURE HOPE'

THIS POEM COMPLETES the story I started in my first book, which was the story of my salvation, and continues on to the present day.

This poem was a lot easier, because it contains a lot more hope for the future, and demonstrates to all just how much we are loved by God, if only we would be willing to give Jesus a chance.

By combining both stories, you will get an overview of my complete life story, and may be encouraged to write your own story of salvation. Since writing this book, I have learned a great deal about book publishing, and especially about myself.

But, overall, my objective has and always will be, salvations, or at least, presenting as many people as I am able to, with a clear cut, thought provoking opportunity, to make a wise and serious decision about their future destination. I pray that you are blessed in abundance as you read, Thank You All,

David T. Gilbert.

Future Hope

I surrendered my life, to Jesus, my Lord,
It was January, 1980, when I encountered God's Word.

The Spirit took me home, to my BessieMae,
It was the time for me, to go home to stay.

In the four Months, BessieMae, and I were as one,
The battle for my soul, was like shifting the sun.

But we made our way through it, we both held on tight,
BessieMae never gave up, though it took all her might.

I went home exhausted, I lost all my fight,
I was not at all well, I slept through the night.

I told her the next morning, what I felt on that day,
She confirmed it was Jesus, by His side, I would stay.

I attended a local Church, one very close by,
The people were so friendly, I was spiritually high.

By November, we moved, up north to settle down,
Elizabeth West was like, a good country town.

We found a little Church, and attended each week,
I was searching for Jesus, so I started to seek.

I thought this small Church, would finally be 'home',
But I felt quite unsettled, so I left there to roam.

About three weeks later, I was contacted again,
It was two elders from 'Klemzig', they came to explain.

One was from a little place, at Prospect, the Church was,
We were there for six years, until we suffered a loss.

My Grandmother was living, at Ethelton, due west,
We would visit each week, she wasn't feeling the best.

We kept up the visits, till the days before she died,
Then we moved to Gawler, we sure loved the countryside.

Gawler was just like, a northern country town,
It was the perfect place, for any man to settle down.

We found a local Church, just a little down the road,
I had proven to the Pastor, I could carry any load.

I first told my story, of salvation at this Church,
I told of my past life, and my eventual re-birth.

Ron was a country Pastor, one I could fully trust,
He saw the gift within me, but fine tune it, I must.

I attended that Church, for one and a half years,
Then I was called to the 'roller drome', I rejoiced with many cheers.

My attendance commenced, from the very first Sunday,
In the year of 1990, I could keep track that way.

By the year of '92, the Church moved down south,
About five mile, to Evanston, where we were building a Spiritual house.

I began serving Jesus, in little jobs at first,
And for His Holy Word, I would hunger and thirst.

My first job was with children, in the babies Creche,
They were quite a little challenge, but I kept with the pace.

I became a 'Home Group Leader', and a good one, too,
I would fascinate the Pastor, 'cause good leaders were few.

For the first year we settled, at Prasards, by the highway,
Our new Church building, was closer to completion each day.

I helped build the new Church, whilst at Prasards Highway Inn,
We could see across the highway, there was excitement within.

I did menial jobs, like emptying the bags,
I was joyful and honoured, using many cleaning rags.

I helped in the kitchen, any way that I could,
I set a good example, as any true leader should.

I did many good things, not refusing anyone,
Serving people, washing dishes, I was having much fun.

I did charity work, helping people in many ways,
I was known as a 'Pillar', who works hard and prays.

I was challenged by the Spirit, to search deep inside,
I had treasure within, good talents, I couldn't hide.

I discovered the gifts, of Encouragement and Strength,
I used them to His Glory, as they were Heaven sent.

I became so talented, at using my Gifts,
My passion was to encourage, speaking words that uplift.

I always seemed filled, with the 'Joy of the Lord',
I was eager to learn, I loved reading God's Word.

I would call people 'Champions', that's what they were to me,
Some wouldn't respond, they were too young to see.

People would be receptive, they loved my special gifts,
They worked especially well, when they needed an uplift.

My objective has always been, for people's salvation,
I started fine tuning, my example, with elation.

I was proven so faithful, I was made kitchen 'Head",
In charge of quite a lot, too much to be said.

It was an enormous honour, to serve God this way,
There was so much to think of, so important to pray.

Then, in September, '05, I visited my Doc,
I was doing strange things, I felt heavy, like a rock.

I couldn't keep my balance, something seemed so wrong,
My signature was tighter, and my feet dragged on.

'I think you have Parkinson's', was his inept reply,
I felt like I had fallen, from way up in the sky.

I didn't quite know, just what to do next,
I was in so much shock, I was so perplexed.

It took about a month, till I knew what to do,
I had two choices, from my point of view.

I could fall in a heap, holding on to my woes,
Or 'stand up and be counted', as the old saying goes.

I was considered a 'Champion', by all of my friends,
They would all stand beside me, being faithful to the end.

I decided to be brave, and defiantly strong,
I would not yield an inch, to do so was wrong.

I know God is with me, His Angels I see,
They surround me daily, and ever watch over me.

I never told my workmates, til I had no choice,
They all suspected something, the sign was in my voice.

In October, '09, the bad news was a shock,
They knew they would lose, a 'Champion' and a Rock.

I lasted another year, then my work would end,
I said farewell to all, on Jesus, I now depend.

This brings things to date, my story has been told,
I trust you will be encouraged, to stand up and be bold.

We have our own story, we need to face our past,
Jesus loves you as you are, He answers prayer fast.

No one sins to a level, where they can't be forgiven,
Jesus died for your sins, in three days, He was risen.

He knew before His death, He'd not die in vain,
For those who believe, He's coming back again.

You have tried life your way, it doesn't work out well,
I would rather be with Jesus, than spend life in hell.

Written and Edited, 13/ 4/ 2011, by David T. Gilbert.

INTRODUCTION TO 'BEYOND MY SALVATION STORY'

THIS IS NOW the second book I have written, and to follow on from the last book, I had the idea of continuing on from where I left off with 'My Moment of Truth'. There were minor details that I omitted to mention, but were still a vital part of my life that needed to be told, in order to fully understand my story.

This poem deals with the psychological and mental strain of recalling the past to mind, and, as a result, having to face the sins of my past once again.

I realize that dwelling on the past has the potential to hinder my walk with Jesus, so I found the necessity to move on from the past and focus on what God would really have me do, because no matter how horrid or sinful our past has been, we need to realize that we have been bought with a price, set free by His Grace, and now we live our lives to serve and please our God, not ourselves.

I pray above all else, that you will be blessed as you read the poetry within,

Thank You All,
David T. Gilbert.

Beyond My Salvation Story

This is the first poem written, in what is my second book,
I trust that you enjoyed my first, and thought it worth having a look.

I missed a few important points, as I was writing my 'Story'.
Although they seemed minor details, they still give God the glory.

My first book was as the Spirit instructed, facing many of my past fears,
Dealing with sins long gone, very often shedding tears.

But there were also good times , it wasn't all doom and sin,
I had good intentions deep inside, but my rebellion controlled me within.

It's quite a challenge, so it pays to be brave, to confront your life of shame,
Three important points, forgive, be accountable, and confess that you're to blame.

These are the obstacles that I faced, as I responded to the challenge,
I had to think, deep and honest, and write the truth as it happened.

The story I wrote was truly fact, without a word of a lie,
Everything happened, as it was told, these facts I couldn't deny.

The places mentioned, people and events, things important to me,
They helped me write my story complete, and opened my eyes to see.

After each poem was completed and done, I gave it to friends to review,
They gave me an honest opinion, of what their thoughts were too.

They all seemed to agree as one, that my poetry was world class art,
The one thing they noted, and all agreed, this poetry came straight from the heart.

I have moved on from the sins of my past, I was forgiven by God above,
I was washed in the blood of the Lamb, and now, I walk in His love.

God does not want us looking back, but at times, it is for a need,
To help us understand His love, and by His Grace, we've been freed.

Our past should never hold us back, from doing what God called us for,
To spread the Good News to one and all, the salvation God offers is sure.

If we use our past to encourage others, telling of God's Amazing Grace,
We reveal to the world a God of love, who died for the human race.

No-one needs a lost eternity, where they taste of the fires of hell,
Time is short, there is still time, before the final bell.

We all have been given a choice, to decide where we finally stand,
Living for pleasure, as goes the world, or being safe in God's hand.

Today, I serve the Lord above, having dealt with my sin and shame,
I have a great deal to be thankful for, and am blessed, in Jesus name.

I now have more to live for, than at any time of my life,
My friends truly love me, God even hand picked my Wife.

My Bessiemae is everything, she's surely a wife, so rare,
She is like a treasure chest of jewels, far too many to bear.

The gifts are encouragement and strength, I have practiced these gifts for years,
Now, I can add one more talent, poetry that could bring folk to tears.

I trust this poem has encouraged you, and inspired you into action,
To look unto Jesus, the God of all Grace, His love will bring satisfaction.

The amazing grace He offers, and to know His peace within,
Is better than all the world could contain, living a life of sin.

INTRODUCTION TO 'A WALKING MIRACLE'

IN THIS POEM, I chose to write of unfathomable gratitude to my God for all He has done in my life, and how He, by His eternal Grace, has lifted me to heights I never could imagine possible. I feel as though I have been highly esteemed and honoured above all, and stand as if among giants (spiritually). Truly, there has never been a day go by, since I surrendered to God, that I don't give a thought to that day in Semaphore when I encountered Jesus, The impact He had on my life was so amazing, no words could adequately describe that encounter, it was just so over-whelming. As an additional result of my surrender to Him, I have seen some of the most awesome miracles that anyone could ever imagine.

Some of the miracles I have seen when I was putting together my first book, only the most privileged of God's servants were likely to see, meaning that I, and only by God's unfathomable Grace, have been highly honoured and immensely privileged to have experienced the power and presence of the Spirit, in the way that I have. To think that I was just one step, literally, from hell, and today, I am able to look back and bring to memory all those lives that I, as a servant of God, have impacted for His Glory, that is a miracle worth noting.

I pray that as you read, you will fall in love with Jesus also, and come to know what it is like to be held safely in His arms, while other lives are seemingly falling to pieces around you. May God richly bless all who read this poem,

David T. Gilbert.

A Walking Miracle

I am so overwhelmed and amazed,
By the saving Grace of God,
He knew everything I'd do in life,
And every place my feet trod.

Before He put the stars in their place,
He had a plan for me,
He knew I would push my life too far,
To the edge of eternity.

But He chose to die for me, anyway,
Breaking satan's sinful spell,
I pushed my life right to the brink,
I was glaring deep into hell,

I had to stop and think that day,
I had gone almost too far,
The only possible hope for me,
Was in the One who created the Stars.

If I had said 'No' to God that day,
My life would have had a swift end,
But I wisely responded to His call,
He remains my Faithful Friend.

Ever since that awesome, golden day,

I am surrendered to His love,

He draws out treasure, deep within,

I faithfully serve God above.

For 31 years, I have walked with God,

I'm a miracle , some people say,

Protected by His Holy Angels,

With His Spirit leading my way.

I have never felt a love so strong,

It reaches to your soul,

The peace you feel inside your heart,

Like a fire in Winters cold.

To think I came so close to death,

I was almost eternally lost,

I have now lived all those extra years,

Reaching souls at any cost.

My gifts are 'Strength' and 'Encouragement',

I use these for His Glory,

Before, I was on my way to hell,

Now I tell a different story.

I am so overwhelmed at times,

He surrounds me by His Grace,

No matter how much I mess up,

I keep running to win my race.

He floods me with His love each morn,
New Mercies ever abound,
I stand in awe of my Holy God,
Like standing on 'Hallowed' ground.

He lifts my spirit above the clouds,
I soar on 'Eagles Wings',
I feel so privileged to be with Him,
My soul breaks forth and sings.

I am so unworthy of His Grace,
I'm a sinful man, at best,
But I place my trust in His Pure love,
And His Faithfulness.

In all the years I have known my Lord,
He has always watched over me,
My passion is to please my Lord,
By being all He'd have me to be.

The miracles I have seen in life,
Straight from God's Holy hand,
Opening doors that were never there,
Turning mountains into sand.

Parting the 'Red Sea' with a blast from His nose,
Saving His children from the fire,
Raising up 'Mighty Men Of Faith',
Granting His servants their desire.

I have noted for my very self,
Mighty moves of the Holy Spirit,
'You can't keep a CHAMPION down' for long,
You must keep running to win it.

Many times, I have seen God hold back time,
Situations, happenings and events,
His hand moving with split second timing,
It's so awesome to be in His presence.

He displays His creative Character,
In the nature of all things,
He's the reason why dolphins jump for joy,
And all of bird life sings.

I serve a Holy, Sovereign God,
All creation is subject to Him,
He is ever seated on the Throne,
His Spirit dwells within.

Of all the people on this earth,
He personally selected me,
He cleansed me with the blood of Jesus,
Then opened my eyes to see.

He raised me up to live for Him,
To be a Champion for His cause,
My desire is to display His love to all,
I respectfully stand before.

I've learned so much about my life,
And the changes made within,
I now know, when it comes to God,
His love keeps me from sin.

We assume that we will rise each morn,
To greet another day,
But God holds all life in His hands,
He has the final say.

We serve a Holy, Sovereign God,
Yet we have the right to choose,
If we choose Christ Jesus, then we surely win,
If not, we are destined to lose.

This poem has reached it's final verse,
And now, you must decide,
It's life or death, the choice is yours,
With my Saviour, I'll ever abide.

INTRODUCTION TO 'PAST ATTITUDES'

In this poem, I describe the recalling of my attitudes of the past, as I was putting together my life story, and the reasons why some attitudes we have in life are not worth holding on to. This is due to certain attitudes being more destructive than productive, and as an afterthought, one thing I have found to be undoubtedly true, is the attitude one displays toward others says more than one thinks about the attitude one has toward ones self! Think on it!

Thank you all for your love and support,

David T. Gilbert.

Past Attitudes

As I was challenged, to write my life story,
I knew it would be, to God's eternal Glory.

I had to return to, and recall the past,
Remembering it all, was a challenging task.

The hurts and mistakes, bitterness and anger,
The risks I took, placing others in danger.

There was so much to think of, so much to recall,
Every minute detail, of my rise and fall.

This was the first time, I'd been challenged this way,
But God had a purpose, and plan for that day.

I had a unique talent, that lay dormant for years,
I wrote from the heart, facing all my fears.

The poetic gift, that I had inside me,
Would be able to open, blind eyes to see.

The Mercy and Love, of an eternal God,
For people He created, through His Holy Word.

In 1980, I was called to His side,
Casting away my arrogance, and my foolish pride.

For years, I had served Him, so faithfully,
Doing menial tasks, all for God's Glory.

I was an example, of His Loving Grace,
Showing God's love, in many a place.

I faced many trials, my faith often tested,
But I was at peace, with where my faith rested.

I had proven my worth, and my loyalty,
I belonged to Jesus, a child of Royalty.

I was a Pillar in the Temple, of my saviour God,
I was Faithful in Tithing, honouring His Word.

I had seen many miracles, and gifts of Healing,
To see God move, was an Awesome feeling.

Then came the day, my Lord challenged me,
To write of my life, so the blind would see.

Our God reveals, His loving heart,
Toward all mankind, offering all a new start.

But there was one point, that I overlooked,
One I forgot to write, in my first book.

It was why I hated, my Dad for so long,
I always blamed him, but I knew I was wrong.

This hatred was from, my low self esteem,
I hated myself, I wanted to scream.

I felt so ugly, from deep inside,
I resented myself, I wanted to hide.

I looked so repulsive, I had little respect,
For who God created, I was just a reject.

I destroyed any photo, I could find of me,
There was no real beauty, that I could ever see.

This was how I felt, of myself back then,
I used it against others, time and again.

I would be so selfish, only my pain mattered,
I was acting a fool, my family felt shattered.

My mood was too much, I pushed friends away,
I was destroying my life, until that Sunday,

When I encountered the God , of heaven above,
He filled me with Joy, and revealed His great love.

He gave me a heart, one like brand new,
He wiped away bitterness, and all hatred too.

I hurt many friends, and I felt so ashamed,
It wasn't their fault, only I was to blame.

In telling my story, I appeal to you all,
Don't be angry, don't hate, these will make you fall.

Hatred is like cancer, it destroys you within,
It's a resident evil, and will cause you to sin.

Bitterness will drive, your friends away,
You will end up having, very little to say.

As I willingly gave, my Lord Jesus all,
He reached out to save me, from my tragic fall.

These days I would rather, bless and love folk,
Now people call me, a pretty good bloke.

The Bible says, 'as you sow, so shall you reap',
This scripture will bring joy, or make your heart weep.

Of all the lost souls that walk this earth,
It is you He chose, to be for rebirth.

It matters little if, of the world, you're a part,
What matters to God, is what's in your heart.

You may think you're a loser, as I often did,
But you are loved by God, He wants you His kid.

If you have any anger, and bitterness too,
The one you will hurt, will be only you.

But if you have a loving, compassionate heart,
You'll never be lonely, and never fall apart.

Those people who display, an attitude to all,
Will face our Saviour, only to fall.

God knew you when, He called you aside,
You are not a loser, so open your heart wide.

He created you to win, to succeed, not fail,
You were created the head, not the wagging tail.

I have learned from experience, the damage done,
When we hold resentment, toward everyone.

When we harbour a heart, filled with trouble and strife,
It does have the means, to shorten your life.

Nobody should live, a life of regret,
We're to deal with our past, then just simply forget.

It becomes a tragedy, when we hold to our past,
Making so much anger, and bitterness last.

We must let go, keep moving ahead,
The past has long gone, time to bury the dead.

To be so positive, letting go of offences,
Is quite a challenge, when you come to your senses.

There are those who will try, to get you real mad,
They are not worth the effort, their attitude is bad.

You need good friends, to brighten your day,
Those who stand with you, along your way.

Who love and support you, in your hard plight,
And who understand when, you had a bad night.

So I encourage you all, as you exit the door,
Always go the extra mile, just to be sure.

If you're like a rock, in attitude and mind,
Having not a friend, only loneliness you find,

Then, take a good look, before it's too late,
Your attitude may be to blame, and not that of your mate.

Your opinion of yourself, it does really matter,
Because no friendship is built, on senseless chatter.

You must be positive, if you want a good friend,
Not holding offence, forgiving to the end.

There are things to ignore, or they get worse,
It is better to bless, than it is to curse.

So, I trust this poem will help you embrace,
Many a good friend, that's no disgrace.

We may meet in Heaven, one future day,
I hope it will be, in a favourable way.

Until that day comes, I bid thee farewell,
Then we will both have, a good story to tell.

David T. Gilbert.

DEDICATION

WHILE THERE ARE some poetry items that are dedicated to certain individuals, this book is dedicated as a whole to the two women who have impacted my life in such an awesome way that, if it wasn't for their input and influence, my story may never have been told, and my life would have been tragically cut short. I am writing of course, about my Mother and my BessieMae.

My Mother was an old fashioned Australian, adhering to Church of England morality and Holy guidelines, and living her life solely for her Children. She was proud of her achievements, loving and protective toward her children, charitable and receptive to most that she met, and hid many painful experiences and secret heartaches and disappointments. But she also knew what it was to sacrifice for her young, but sadly, her life was cut short all too soon, and before she had a chance to live as she dreamed, God took her home.

As for my BessieMae, she has been my strength, sanity, guardian, companion, friend, critic, guide, eyes and ears, in fact, I would dare to say that she deserves as much recognition for the putting together of this book as I do. She has done a lot of work behind the scenes, with very little, if any recognition at all, and without her, this book would never have seen the light of a bookshelf in any store. I will forever be in debited to her for her faith in me, and her love for me, not to mention her support in what I have taken up as a challenge.

I am so excited about the future hope that I have, that one day soon, all three of us will meet again in Heaven, and with us will be those we have managed to encourage to be saved through our team efforts in publishing our work, and doing our part to spread the Gospel Message all over our dying world, God richly bless you all,

David T. Gilbert, BessieMae Gilbert, Fay Minnetta Mabel Gilbert.
(Deceased.).

INTRODUCTION TO 'MY MOTHER, MY FRIEND"

AFTER WRITING AND publishing my first book, My Moment Of Truth, I set about to put into poetry a lot of the emotional side of my life, such as, what did I learn, if anything, from the terrible bungles and mistakes that I made at that time? What were my views about life in general? And what evidence, if any, was there of any such changes? I tried my best to cover as much of my life as possible, in relating to the above areas, but the one person I had almost forgotten, who played such a major role in my story, was my Mum.

Her death played such an enormous role in my surrendering to Christ, that if I did not write a mention about her, I would be completely negligent in my honour of her. Mum was no shining light for Australia in any way, or to any degree, but the life she lived was too short, and was over far too soon, but even though she never did get to see her oldest son and friend marry, through a sheer miracle of God, she did get the chance to see her future 'Daughter-in-law' prior to her death. It still amazes me to this day, the amazing wisdom of God in knowing what we are destined to do in life, who we are to partner with, and even knowing the final outcome of our lives, long before we ever realize that there is a God who loves us, far beyond any length of our understanding. God knows our fears, concerns, what makes us happy, what we are liable to do, and that on any given day, and at any given time, He knows more about us than we could ever comprehend, if only we would put our trust in the One nobody could ever hope to out—love.

My prayer to you all, is that you may somehow be able to relate to what I have written, and duly honour those Mothers that are never really appreciated enough for the sacrifices they make for the ones they love the most. Mothers of the world, I honour you and salute you for all that you do toward your children, may God richly bless you all,

David T. Gilbert.

My Mum, My Friend

It was just over thirty three years ago,
That my Mother had passed away,
My memory of her, still fresh in my mind,
As if it were yesterday.

She lived a short, but tragic life,
Cancer was the cause of her end,
To me, she was more than just my Mum,
I knew her as a personal friend.

She saw me as a tower of strength,
A safe haven, in stormy weather,
We would talk for hours, on the troubles she had,
Her secrets remain safe, forever.

The pain that she lived with, most of her life,
I came to fully understand,
Was due to many unwise and bemused choices,
Which was not in line with God's plan!

Mum never achieved anything notable in life,
She made no great name for herself,
She never won gold or silver for Australia,
And she was never lavished with ample wealth.

But she was my Mum, and I loved her so much,
I saw some of the pain she endured,
Perceiving her emotions, like a timely friend,
She bore fears that needed a cure.

She was a woman of undeniable courage,
Who, for her children, would lay down her life,
She possessed an inner dignity and charm,
Unique, in such a faithful wife.

Mum was quite strict on moral discipline,
Imparting her values into us all,
Her focus was for us to marry for the good,
So our families would help us stand tall.

But the sacrifices she made for her beloved kids,
Just to make it in life another day,
Helped me to believe in, and love her so much,
Her actions spoke more than she could say.

Mum had an emotional side to her,
Caring for the things that mattered,
She was the one holding our family together,
After her passing on, we just simply scattered.

For a number of years, there was little contact,
We all had to learn a new life,
But there was good news amid the bad,
As I led my two Brothers to Christ.

I wasn't saved, when Mum was cremated,
But that didn't phase God at all,
Through His eyes, I saw Mum's radiant face,
I was awestruck, as I still recall.

That glow I saw, upon her still face,
Took me by complete surprise,
It was a look of total, absolute peace,
The one thing missing from her life.

I was so confused, I just couldn't comprehend,
Why she was called home, still being young,
Her day came earlier than most others did,
To me, it was unfair and quite wrong.

But I never realised God's perfect, Divine plan,
He was answering my Mum's final prayer,
She wanted to seen her best friend's bride,
Or at least, by his side, who'd be there.

It wasn't till after I surrendered to Christ,
That my BessieMae told me a story,
Of how she had a Divine appointment,
To bring Jesus tremendous Glory.

She was taking her Son to the Hospital,
But accidentally caught the wrong bus,
But she never realised how Divine it was,
There was a reason for all the fuss.

God knew I would miss, my only real chance,
To introduce my future bride to my Mum,
So God did the one thing, I could never do,
Mum saw my bride, then surrendered to the Son.

My Mum loved God, in her early, younger years,
But family challenges steered her away,
So, my BessieMae told Mum about the Lord,
And her hope, for a better day.

When I was told that story, as fact,
The Spirit of God announced with glee,
Your Mum awaits you in Heaven above,
There was exaltation inside of me.

And now, I await the return of my Lord,
His wisdom astounds me still,
To think He knew, before the creation,
Mum's prayer, He would easily fulfil.

If you are able to relate to this story, as told,
Knowing you love your Mum as I do,
Then go on, give her a big, loving hug,
Telling her what she means to you.

David T. Gilbert.

INTRODUCTION TO 'THIRTY TWO YEARS TOGETHER'

This poem is not only based on factual events, but is a heart-felt dedication to my wife of 31 years, this November, 22, but we have been as one since October, 10, 1979. Taking on a ready made Family is quite a challenge, at the best of times, but when an individual knows beyond all reasoning, that their soul mate stands right before their eyes, only a total fool would walk away from the opportunity of a life time. I am still so passionately in love with my BessieMae, that I feel as though I am only half a man without her, even after these past years. So if any of you women love to be romanced, by that knight in shining armour that you married all those years ago, direct your other half toward this poem, asking if he could just once be bold, and captivate your heart once again, as my BessieMae has captivated mine.

May God bless all who read this work of passion,

David T. Gilbert.

'Thirty Two Years Together'

I still recall the very first time,
I looked upon your countenance,
You appeared as a beauty, so Divine,
I just had to take a second glance.

My heart was captivated in a moment,
I somehow knew, you would be mine,
It was just as if, you were Heaven sent,
Chosen for me, at just the right time.

I first came to know you as a friend,
We would sit, and talk for hours,
Your wisdom flowed against the trend,
Your simplicity was like Summer showers.

I found I couldn't let you pass by,
This moment was just too good to miss,
To me, you were of a class, so high,
Just to be in your presence was bliss.

The challenge for me, was already there,
Your children needed two Parents,
Taking on Family is at times, hard to bear,
But I couldn't walk from your presence.

To me, you were just, too good to be true,

Like a chest of jewels, silver and gold,

Each time I dug deep, I'd find something new,

Like beholding a fire, in Winter's cold.

You became to me, a tower of strength,

You taught me so much about life,

You fascinated me, as we talked at length,

I just had to make you my Wife.

At times, your simplicity was child-like,

As an infant on any Christmas eve,

You knew how to keep your attitude right,

And you taught me how to truly believe.

It was you who helped me find Jesus above,

You patiently waited for me,

You were His gift, Given to me with love,

Now at last, I am totally free.

The plan that He had for us both,

Has lasted almost 32 years,

Looking back on those times, we can joyfully boast,

And maybe shed, a few joyful tears.

The timing you had, was perfect and right,

Knowing somehow, when to let go,

I'm so passionate for you, day and night,

You're a woman I am privileged to know.

You were all that I desired in a wife,
But over time, I found much more,
I am so highly honoured, having you in my life,
You're the one woman I would die for.

I am abundantly blessed by my Lord above,
Words could never adequately say,
Just how sheltered I feel, in His arms of love,
He is the Truth, the Life, the Way.

After the life I had, before I was saved,
Compared to the life I live now,
Is just like being risen from the grave,
And starting afresh, some how.

So if you have a desire to truly live,
And have your marriage full of passion,
Come to Jesus, He will love and forgive,
And refire you in a Heavenly fashion.

INTRODUCTION TO 'SALVATION IS . . .'

IN THIS POEM, I write down my thoughts on the subject of Salvation.

As I have written before, I prefer to write about factual experiences rather than anything fictional or dreamed up. If it happened in my life, I will write about it, because when one writes about actual events they have experienced, you know that their work is coming from deep within, from the heart.

I have tried very hard to write my poetry in such a way that it doesn't repeat the same story over, but tells a similar story from multiple angles, covering as many views as possible that could be considered vital to understanding the story that is told as the full story.

My work in this poem is a combination of my own experiences, and what God's Word says about the subject, and was scrutinized by Pastoral friends of mine, as I wanted this to be as accurate as can be. I trust you will be able to relate to some of what is noted, being wonderfully blessed as you read,

Yours in Christ,
David T. Gilbert.

Salvation is . . .

Salvation is God's Holy Plan,

    To save the soul of sinful man,

        Having faith in the sacrifice of God's only Son,

He paid a debt He did not owe,

    Suffering at the hands of an evil foe,

        The battle for man's salvation was almost won.

Three days later, Jesus rose again,

    In victory over sin and shame,

        The empty tomb was the evidence, of His victory.

He suffered in His body, to pay our debt,

    So that we may remember, and never forget,

        The blood He shed on that cross, just to set us free.

And now, due to His sacrifice,

    We all must come to realize,

        We need not live in bondage anymore,

By Jesus blood, we've been set free,

    To live with Him eternally,

        The Saints will come from every distant shore.

I still reminisce about that day,

   When Jesus met me on my way,

      He revealed to me His Love, His Peace and Grace.

That day is one I could not forget,

   I accepted Him without regret,

      And now, I find I'm running a different race.

I have grown and come so far since then,

   And still, I can reflect on when,

      God moved so strong and mighty in my life.

The miracles and changes that I saw,

   And moves of the Spirit, not seen before,

      It was good to live without trouble, and without strife.

When you receive His Saving Grace,

   It's just like starting a marathon race,

      You will find there are many obstacles in your way.

Things that will try and make you fall,

   Or fool you into thinking small,

      Just keep on moving forward to 'The Day'.

At times, the going gets quite tough,

   You feel as though you've had enough,

      But Jesus is there with you by your side.

He is your Defence, your Strength and Shield,

We never say die, we dare not yield,

There is no turning back, we will not hide.

God's Kingdom is not of this earth,

Salvation is by God's planned rebirth,

By His Amazing Grace, we are born again.

We live a new life to our Lord,

One that's according to His Word,

Never turning back to a life of sin and shame.

We are called to be 'Ambassadors' for Him,

Rescuing lives from worldly sin,

Winning souls is what this life is all about.

We walk in obedience to our God,

Spreading the Good news of His Word,

On the Day of His return, there will be a Victory shout.

The example we set before our neighbour,

To encourage and show, we have God's favour,

These things should be an important point in mind.

We live a Holy life by Grace,

Our precious time we dare not waste,

Making the most of opportunities every time.

Miracles of Healing, will He do,

    Through humble folk, like me and you,

        Obeying the very least of His commands.

Having no confidence in our flesh,

    Because our way ends in a mess,

        Our trust we place in Jesus' worthy hands.

Our hope is the foundation of our Faith,

    God's promises are true, they're ours by Grace,

        God is so Holy, no one compares to Him.

With God, our trust is based on Truth,

    The Holy Spirit is living proof,

        Of a future life with God, and His Cherubim.

Salvation means that and so much more,

    Jesus is knocking on your hearts door,

        So open up and receive the Saviour now.

He will forgive you of your sin,

    He'll renew your life from deep within,

        His Spirit of Truth, will guide and teach you how.

As we hearken to the Spirits voice,

    He challenges us to make a choice,

        Obey the Spirit, or yield to worldly sin.

The Spirit won't force His right of way,

    Some decisions we make, we need first 'Pray',

        Listening to the voice of Wisdom within.

But Jesus knows the way we live,

    He knows there's freedom, when we forgive,

        We are like precious jewels in His Holy hand.

We study and read His Word each day,

    Eagerly finding the time to pray,

        The Tithe is based on principle, not command.

Since Jesus Christ first set me free,

    I walk by faith in His victory,

        Living my life as described in His Holy Word.

New mercies greet me every day,

    Helping me on my joyful way,

        God's voice is the sweetest sound ever to be heard.

My aim is to tell everyone I see,

    Of how I walk in His victory,

        With my Faithful Saviour leading all the way.

He will always be my Number one,

    By His Grace, I'll live to Praise God's Son,

        I joyfully look ahead toward 'The Day'.

Forgive and Forget

Quote: The offences we overlook today will impact on our attitudes of tomorrow.

If you look in the Bible, with Spiritual eyes,
You will soon discover, life is full of surprise,
It's not that clean cut, for everyone,
For most of us though, we need God's wisdom.

To love one another, as only Jesus could love,
Is not of this world, but from God up above,
Love helps you forgive, your Sister and Brother,
It binds us in unity, to support one another.

When people offend you, or cause you great pain,
Drive you to your limits, time and again,
Do unto them, as Jesus would do,
Forgive and forget, as He did to you.

Some people offend you, before your very face,
Others falsely accuse you, treating you with disgrace,
Even those who befriend you, declaring love for their Brother,
Under pressure will deny you, then go running for cover.

It is in our nature, to do harm to our kin,

Exercising revenge, just to score even,

Sin is aggressive, thinking only of self,

Shortening your life, and causing ill health.

There are those in the Bible, whose lives were an influence,

A timely example, of how not to take offence,

They endured injustice, ridicule and shame,

Keeping their lives focused, for God's Glorious Name.

The example they set, showing how we should live,

Urges us to show mercy, and be ready to forgive,

They showed no bitterness, but exercised faith,

In the one they know, as the God of all Grace.

There was Noah, so humble, who dared to obey,

Enduring ridicule and jest, right up to the day,

That God sealed the ark, sending forth the flood,

The world was then cleansed, without shedding blood.

Abraham stood in faith, trusting in God's Word,

When asked to sacrifice his Son, he obeyed what he heard,

His obedience was rewarded, he received back his Son,

Anointed the 'Father of All Nations', by Heaven's Holy One.

Then Jacob wrestled vigorously, all night with God,

He obtained the promise, keeping hold of His Word,

Joseph was the victim, of his jealous Brothers,

Sold as a slave, cause he was different from the others.

He was taken to Egypt, where a slave he would be,
But he wouldn't let go, of his integrity,
He was falsely accused, by Potiphar's Wife,
Then thrown into jail, she caused him much strife.

God's anointing was with him, so was His favour,
He was put in complete control, of prison by his jailer,
He interpreted dreams, as no one else could,
Warned Pharoah of future turmoil, avoid it, he should.

Pharoah made Joseph, to be second in command,
He brought his entire Family, into a foreign land,
God's plan for Joseph, was to save his kin,
His story inspires us, to seek holiness within.

Then there was Moses, who was saved from slaughter,
Rescued from the reeds, by Pharoah's Daughter,
He was raised an Egyptian, strong, handsome and brave,
But chose living with his kin, as a Hebrew slave.

In the dessert, for forty years, he roamed around,
Until God commanded him, to stand on Holy ground,
He freed his people from bondage, by ten awesome plagues,
It was the time God's might, in Egypt was displayed.

The Hebrews came out laden, with Egyptian treasure,
God dealt them a blow, to their life of pleasure,
Moses lowered his staff, to part the Red S ea,
That truly would have been, an awesome sight to see,

The cloud by day, and the fire by night,
Guided the Hebrew nation, till their land was in sight,
But when they finally reached, the promised Holy land,
Of the twelve, only two, had faith in God's plan.

The end result for them, was a forty year trek,
That generation perished, giving them time to reflect,
On what could have been, a life of God's blessing,
But they chose instead, a life so depressing.

Joshua led his people, into the promised land,
His integrity remaining firm, as he yielded to God's command,
At Jericho, Joshua had not the slightest doubt,
When the walls were flattened, by a single SHOUT.

Gideon was considered, the least of all men,
He rose up in faith, to be God's champion,
He obeyed God's instruction, waiting all night long,
To defeat ten thousand, with just three hundred strong.

Samson was strong, but ended life blind,
He felled the Temple pillars, killing 3,000 Philistines.
David was despised, by his jealous Brothers,
But when Goliath did shout, they all ran for cover.

When David heard Goliath, he spoke up in faith,
He would rid Israel, of their timely disgrace.
With a single small stone, he knocked Mr. Big dead,
Then took his heavy sword, and cut off his head.

Despite his Brother's sarcasm, he stood up and believed,

The Kingship of Israel, is what he received.

Solomon was known, as the wisest of all,

With 700 wives, he was having a ball.

He wrote many Proverbs, wisdom to live by,

But despite his great wisdom, he eventually would die.

Esther risked her life, to protect her people,

The King fell in love, with this beautiful Hebrew.

Ruth was proven faithful, she fought hard and long,

Despite looking poorly, her faith stood out strong,

She was faithful and true, to her new Mistress,

She was destined for history, despite her distress.

Shadrach, Meshach and Abednego,

When commanded to worship, defiantly said 'NO',

They stood loyal to the God, who dwelt much higher,

Walking safely with Him, amidst the raging fire.

Mary was fastidious, making all things look neat,

But Mary sat worshipping, at her Lord Jesus' feet,

Peter asked a question, no other dare quote,

But he was the only soul, to step out of the boat.

There are so many stories, too many to tell,

Of those whose integrity, would keep them from hell,

They never retaliated, but kept showing love,

Forgiving and forgetting, like Jesus above.

So if you think deeply, about the sin we daily do,

Doing our own thing, when we should remain true,

Putting our hand to, what He told us to avoid,

No wonder God sometimes, gets so annoyed.

We beg for forgiveness, for one sin or another,

Then go and curse, our Sister and Brother,

How can we justify, our case before God,

When we are not willing, to live by His Word?

God has called us to, a pure, and Holy life,

In the Kingdom of His Son, without trouble or strife,

He wants us to trust Him, and simply OBEY,

And wants us to walk, in His presence each day.

We should never pre-judge, or condemn one another,

But encourage, support, and love every Brother,

Leaving an example, for the next generation,

So that they will be, the finest in our Nation.

INTRODUCTION TO "CHOICES"

THERE ARE TIMES in our lives, that we often wonder about the effect our being here would have, on people, loved ones, even past and present friendships, some of us even question whether God made the right choice when He called us to His side.

My focus in this poem is to help people see that God most definitely knew who He had hand-picked, when He chose you to be not only a citizen of His Kingdom, but a member of His Royal family. I also intend to help people realize that you all make a difference to people's lives, because it isn't always those things that stand out and get noticed that matter the most , as much as it is the small, unnoticed, hidden things that we take for granted, and assume that we have no value because we are not always in the limelight.

Indeed, most of the greatest heroes of the Bible were mentioned as having come from the most humble of beginnings, like Noah, Abram, Joseph, Shadrach, Meshach and Abednego, David, and so on. Have you ever thought seriously what the world, or even mankind, would have been like if they had not ever have been, would there ever have been a "Promised Land?" Even more terrifyingly chilling is the thought of Jesus never dying on that blood soaked cross, how much of a difference would that have made? There are many more angles to this thought that we could continue on with, but time does not permit, suffice as to say, we need to appreciate who we are in Christ and for what purpose we were called, "making the most of every opportunity", as God's Holy Word says. I pray that you are blessed as you read,

David T. Gilbert.

Choices

Each day, we make choices, with all that we do,
To laugh like a clown, or be sad and blue.

To be angry and violent, to say yes or no,
The choice is ours, whichever way you go.

In the Bible is written, the principles of God,
It's our choice to accept, or reject His pure Word.

I often reflect, upon my sad life,
The trouble I caused, the confusion and strife.

But when I look closer, there's one thing I see,
I can see where my Lord, was watching over me,

Before I ever knew Him, He was there by my side,
Awaiting the right moment, to deal with my pride.

His timing was perfect, and still always is,
At just the right time, He called me to live.

I still fail to see, what He chose me for,
To me, I was unworthy, useless and poor.

I thought He was crazy, out of His mind,
But He knew who He chose, that was proven in time.

When I first encountered, my Lord and Friend,
My life of sin, would soon have it's end.

He gave me a choice, His Kingdom or mine,
To live eternally, or perish with the blind.

I had nothing to live for, I had no real worth,
So I accepted Jesus, and His plan of re-birth.

I have often reflected, on the years since then,
The years I've been serving, faithfully to the end.

The friendships I made, the people I encouraged,
My influence on the youth, my heaven blessed marriage.

What difference would it have made, if I was never there,
Would anyone notice, would anyone really care?

What if Adam hadn't fallen, or yielded to sin,
How different would life be, when would our time end?

If Noah Had said "no", to the Lord that day,
Would all life on earth, have been swept away?

And what about Abram, who was a humble man,
If he had said "no". would there still be a 'Promised Land'?

If Joseph had decided, not to forgive his brothers,
Would Israel have survived, or perish like the others?

If Moses had decided, to enjoy sinful pleasure,
Would there have been an Exodus, of slaves and treasure?

And how about David, if he sat this one out,
Israel would still be wondering, what the fighting was about!

Shadrach, Meshach, and Abednego,
if they yielded to the King, Would they still be heroes?

We could go on for some time, but suffice as to say,
We only get one life, so make a difference today.

You were called to win, so think well of yourself,
God knew what He did, when He called you to Himself.

He chose us to display, His Holy Glory,
To tell the whole world of His salvation story.

Because He chose death, rather than disobey,
We are saved by grace, to praise Him every day.

So, the next time you feel, a little sorry for yourself,
No matter what, get over it, and think of someone else.

There are stories of people, who suffer in pain,
They praise their God, and consider what is to gain.

If you can praise the Lord, despite how you feel,
You will soon discover that, His mercy is for real.

Jesus loves you more, than you could comprehend,
I want to tell the world, His love truly has no end.

So, please consider carefully, the things you've just read,
You matter to God, give Jesus a go instead.

INTRODUCTION TO 'DETERMINED TO WIN'

THIS IS A poem that has been written before, but in a different way, and with a bit more of a personal touch to it. The personal aspect of this poem derives from my desire to write only about those things that are 'fact' in my life, and therefore are straight from my heart. The factual side allows me to write in sincerity and truth, making my work a very personal one, in the sense that one could never dispute my work to any degree, because what is written is exactly what I experienced personally. I have made this poem as detailed as I was able to do, without going into too much melodrama, as it deals with my emotions at the latest stage of my life, and the hidden fears that most of us try to hide.

The God aspect of the poem is in relation to the One person I have been able to rely on, as I have been battling this disease, the One person that has always been beside me 24/7, revealing Himself as totally Faithful, my friend, the Holy Spirit. Without Him by my side, life would be almost impossible to cope with, so I pray that you will be blessed as you read,

David T. Gilbert.

'Determined To Win'

Parkinson's Disease is the greatest challenge,
That I have ever had to face,
Each day is like a battle for life,
A continual struggle, to finish my race.

The jobs and tasks that I used to do,
Seem now like a by-gone dream,
Each Winter is a season I annually dread,
The struggle sometimes makes me scream.

But, I serve a faithful God above,
His love is evident all around,
He has sustained me by way of His Holy hand,
I feel I'm standing on Holy ground.

My wife has been such a strength to me,
And so understanding of my affliction,
She has tolerated a lot since first diagnosed,
I'm so thankful for her loving affection.

I have written down my experiences with this,
In the hope of supporting all folk,
To understand that this restrictive disease,
Won't stop me from passing on some hope.

Each time I call out to God in prayer,

He faithfully answers my cry,

I feel so secure in His arms of love,

Without Him, I would surely die.

God assists me in my daily struggles,

To rise with every new dawn,

His grace blesses me, and keeps me safe,

I'm very grateful for every new morn.

His encouragement is ever there for me,

He protects me in every case,

It only makes me much more determined,

To want to finish my race.

I know I can't give up on life too soon,

That option has no actual appeal,

I have so many who honour me, and support me in prayer,

Greatly blessed is how I really feel.

There are times when I feel so drained and flat,

There is always the question, 'Why',

But, I know this world is full of sin,

And it will eventually die.

I try not to linger on this restrictive disease,

There are others worse off than me,

I put my mind on others instead,

And pray God keeps them free.

At first, my energy began to fade,

And I couldn't stand up straight,

My signature became tight and small,

And I shuffled in my walk of late.

Sexual performance diminished in time,

My speech would be like a muffle,

The words I spoke began to slur,

My days became more of a struggle.

My medication at first, really spun me out,

My body had to adjust to change,

My stamina began to slow me down,

At work, I felt quite strange.

From my first diagnosis, to the day I left work,

The span was about four years,

I took all my sick leave and R. D. O.'s,

I had to stand tall amid my fears.

I spent a week in hospital, once,

I had pneumonia quite bad,

I sent confusion amongst the staff,

Due to the medication I had.

My medication had to be so precise,

Right down to within a minute,

Unlike medications that other patients took,

Precision was essential to beat it.

There are also days of changing weather,
I could tell up to two days before,
I have also lost sixteen kilos in weight,
Due to the medication I endure.

After Four years, I really felt the cold,
I lost most of my muscle fat,
My body looked like a 'bag of bones',
And in my face, I reflected that.

By now, I was on a high dose of pills,
As I stood, my body would sway,
At night, my limbs would spasm and twitch,
This was due to having a bad day.

My God has sustained me quite well, so far,
He has been a most faithful friend,
He has shown much mercy and grace to me,
His love endures to no end.

I have been so blessed in many awesome ways,
My friends remain supportive and true,
I have been given more chances to live my dreams,
Than most other people ever do.

I have published a book about my salvation,
It is titled, 'My Moment Of Truth',
It is a good tool for the saving of souls,
In heaven, I will see the actual proof.

I trust this poem will assist many people,
In understanding my restrictive plight,
In any case, I am determined to win,
I will never give up the fight.

But as I look back into the history of my life,
My mind dwells on one thing, so sad,
I was once the strength of so many in strife,
Urging them to thank God for what they had.

I would work so hard at serving the Lord,
I did many tasks other folk wouldn't do,
I could never say 'no', and my Wife showed concern,
'One day, they will be the death of you'!

I rarely heeded the warnings she spoke,
To me, I was serving my Saviour,
I would faithfully work, to provide for my kin,
Many times, in the light of God's favour.

The sacrifices I made, to keep them well fed,
Gave me a really good reputation,
I was a prime example of a devoted family man,
One of the finest in the whole Nation.

I was honoured by all, with loving affection,
My attitude was one to be desired,
My conduct and example, were second to none,
In worship, I would really be on fire.

But since this disease had taken it's cruel hold,
I could only reminisc of passed days,
I'm totally at the mercy of God above,
Yet, He faithfully provides in many ways.

It seems so sad, that I have been afflicted,
After being so faithful to so many,
It's me that needs the support, this time,
It makes my heart feel so heavy.

I know the time will come one day,
When I may end up wheelchair bound,
I would prefer to bow out of life with a BANG,
Than quietly depart without a sound.

To explain, I would rather be remembered,
For all the good I did for others,
Encouraging them all, by being an example,
Of love, to my Sisters and Brothers.

But I really shouldn't be that concerned,
What would actually concern me the most,
Is, on the day, when Jesus returns for His Bride,
I am forgotten by the Holy Ghost.

Until that day comes, I will do my utmost,
To be the best example to all,
I want to be accountable, for all the good I did,
Working to hear, my Saviour's call.

Dedicated to all sufferers of Parkinson's Disease,
Their Carers, the Medical Staff who treat them,
The Medical Researchers trying to find a cure,
And anyone else I may have missed who is
Associated with this disease,

May The God Of All Creation Bless You,
Keep You Safe, And Grant You The
Support, Help And Assistance That
Most People Are Reluctant To Give,
Due To A Lack Of Understanding.

God Knows Who The Real HEROES Of This
Crumbling World Are,
Thank You All, Jesus Loves YOU!

David T. Gilbert.

INTRODUCTION TO 'OH, WHAT AN AWESOME GOD'

IN THIS POEM, I wrote these words for 2 reasons, firstly, to express my appreciation to God for all He has done, and all He is to me, and secondly, as a call to all who read this poem, that time is so short, and we need to urgently get ready for the return of our Lord this day, and not put it off until tomorrow. According to the signs stated in the Bible, Jesus may return for His Bride much sooner than you think. If He did, are you ready for heaven, or is there any shadow of doubt? Read and meditate,

Your Friend in Christ,
David T. Gilbert.

Oh, What An AWESOME GOD!

My God is so faithful, and loving to me,
   He showed His great love, at Calvary,
      Then opened my eyes, that I may see,
Oh, what an Awesome God!

His grace is amazing, He is the best,
   His Kingdom is the only place to invest,
      In His loving arms, we will find rest,
Oh, what a Gracious God!

His Holy Angels obey as He speaks,
   In His Righteous Ones, It's obedience He seeks,
      We joyfully serve Him, throughout the weeks,
Oh, what a Holy God!

How do we invest in His Kingdom above?
   By showing Compassion, Forgiveness and Love,
      Revealing His Spirit, God's Snow White Dove,
Oh, what a Loving God!

Our God is Creator, of all you see,
   He even created, you and me,
      The hills, the valleys, the land and the sea
Oh, what a Creative God!

It is to His Glory, we were born this day,
Whether young and pretty, or old and grey,
He called us to live, in a Holy way,
Oh, what a Compassionate God!

For all mankind, did Jesus die,
He gave a choice, to you and I,
Receive His Grace, or live with the lie,
Oh, what a Merciful God!

He is the only true God I know,
He cleanses our hearts, in the crimson flow,
So they are as clean, as pure, white snow,
Oh, what a Beautiful God!

Honour and Favour, are His to impart,
He wants to cleanse, and renew our heart,
And wants to give us, a brand new start,
Oh, what a Forgiving God!

The fruit of the Spirit, for us, He desires,
So we can start spreading the Spirit's Fire,
Throughout this earth, as God requires,
Oh, what an Omnipresent God!

Each morning we arise, it's a brand new day,
New mercies we receive, along our way,
To God, we are Diamonds, in jars of clay,
Oh, what a Priceless God!

Our God resides in the purest Light,
    Unapproachable, it is, just to get it right,
        His Angels watch over us, each day and night,
Oh, what a Righteous God!

My Saviour is my Strength and Shield,
    To any other, I refuse to yield,
        He is our Victory, on the Battlefield,
Oh, what an Omnipotent God!

He comes with healing, in His wings,
    He is to me, my everything,
        And for His Glory, my heart sings,
Oh, what an All Caring God!

Our God has shown us unfathomable Love,
    Pouring down from Heaven above,
        On the gentle wings, of His Snow White Dove,
Oh, what an Infinite God!

He raises up men, of Integrity,
    Opens blind eyes, that they may see,
        Pours out His Blessings, on you and me,
Oh, what a Sovereign God!

I have been so fortunate, throughout my life,
    God's favour rests upon me, and my wife,
        Our marriage has been blessed, with little strife,
Oh, what a Concerning God!

Our Children love us, we know that well,

    We hope to help them, escape this hell,

        Before St. Peter, sounds the final bell,

Oh, what an Amazing God!

After that bell, when it's sound is heard,

    It will be too late, to respond to His Word,

        The Saints would have gone, to be with the Shepherd,

Oh, what a True Judging God!

Not long after that, it will be hell on earth,

    Before it's too late, join the rebirth,

        Value your time, for every second it's worth,

Oh, what a Long Suffering God!

The final call, is getting close,

    So yield your lives, to the Holy Ghost,

        Of your opportunities, you best make the most,

Oh, what a Patient God!

When we see Jesus, riding high,

    Upon the white clouds, way in the sky,

        It will be time for the Saints, to say good bye,

Oh, what a Redeeming God!

On reaching Heaven, we will all rejoice,

    Shouting His praises, all with one voice,

        We are citizens of heaven, by our own choice,

Oh, what a Magnificent God!

What an Awesome day that will be,
    Continuing our lives, in eternity,
        With Jesus our King, what a sight to see,
Oh, what a Praise Worthy God!

But for those left behind, what a day of gloom,
    Having to face a fearful doom,
        Like being buried alive, in a dusty tomb,
Oh, what a Fearful God!

NO god can save you from what happens then,
    The demons of hell are released from their den,
        Your fear will overwhelm you, and you won't find a friend,
Oh, what a Terrifying God!

To escape this fear, there is very little time,
    Make your choice now, before the Bell's chime,
        Otherwise your life won't be worth a dime,
Oh, what a Consuming God!

If this poem's end, fills you with fear,
    Call out to Jesus, while He is still near,
        That final Day draws closer each year,
Oh, what a Tolerant God!

I have my pass, and I await the day,
    I will rejoice evermore, as I hear my Lord say,
        'Well done, faithful servant, your treasure is this way'.
Oh, what an AWESOME GOD!

INTRODUCTION TO 'THE LOVER OF MY LIFE'

THIS POEM IS about one's concept of God before salvation, a realization of our sinful state, and an awakening to the love and com-passion God has for us, and the appreciation to God for all He has done for us. Indeed, we could never thank God adequately, because we have limited knowledge, in the sense that we go by what we are awakened to, but God has done more than we could ever realize. There are many times in our lives that we do not recognise the things that God does for us until after the final outcome is accomplished, then we thank God.

I wrote this poem in a personalised way, as if the reader was address-ing God direct, because God is a personal God, and we need to appre- ciate Him accordingly. Do you love God personally? I know He loves me that way! Be blessed as you read,

David T. Gilbert.

The Lover of My Life

I felt so shameful and unworthy,
When I first encountered You,
I always thought Your love was for,
The privileged, selected few.

I would walk right past Your Holy House,
Each and every Sunday morn,
Heading to where my friends would be,
Arising with the dawn.

Your righteous, Church going people,
Would always look my way,
As if to notion in unison,
'Another wasted day'.

I thought they were looking down at me,
In brazen indignation,
But the reality of their thinking was,
Toward my sad situation.

They seemed so high and unreachable,
I could never be that good,
I thought one had to be squeaky clean,
As everybody else should.

I recall as a younger lad,

My days at Sunday School,

But serving You just seemed so drab,

But being a rebel was so cool.

Some years passed by until I awoke,

And recognised my sin,

You broke those chains that held me down,

And changed my heart within.

You paid my debt in Your own blood,

Your Grace had set me free,

And now, I live for You alone,

And I humbly bow my knee.

Your love is so overwhelming,

So gentle, yet so strong,

I never understood till now,

It's with You that I belong.

The race You marked out for me,

Was planned before creation,

The basic plan is for all people,

From every tribe and nation.

We run according to Your plan,

In humble, total submission,

Being obedient to Your Divine will,

Is proof of our spiritual transition.

We all are given an even chance,

To bear fruit to Your name,

But if we neglect to accept our part,

We will end our days in shame.

I reflected on my sad, tragic life,

Just out of curiosity,

And realized that at many times,

You were watching over me.

Those days long passed, when I was young,

I was full of evil intent,

You were there, right by my side,

No matter where I went.

I would involve myself in mischief,

Causing many lots of pain,

I was so blinded from realizing,

My folly was to my shame.

I should have died at Semaphore,

I pushed life to the limit,

But you gave me a second chance,

And a brand new start, within it.

Since then, You took my sinful heart,

Transforming it to practice good,

I renounced my life of sin and shame,

As any true follower should.

I have never felt so wonderfully free,
Those chains from hell have gone,
By faith, I have Your Holy name,
To build my life upon.

You were there, walking in the garden,
When Adam lost his way,
You were known as Yahweh way back then,
When Adam fell that day.

By the time Moses introduced the Law,
You were known then as 'I AM',
Then David was anointed as Israel's King,
Everything was going to plan.

Then one day, Your star appeared,
Above the stable, in the sky,
Your Son came down, to pay for sin,
A man born, just to die.

You showed Your Love, upon that cross,
I thought I had to be perfect,
Your people looked, so unreceptive,
You seemed too Holy to worship.

He walked amongst us, choosing twelve,
They followed Him for over 3 years,
He taught them Kingdom principles,
And how to walk in Faith, not fear.

He received all, who would come to Him,
Though the Pharisees were annoyed,
They feared Him, 'cause He was the Truth,
His life, they were out to destroy.

He died upon a splintery cross,
After a mockery of a trial,
They violated every Holy law,
Just to suit their arrogant style.

Crucifixion is no joke at all,
It is an inhumane death,
Jesus paid the price for all,
Right up to His last breath.

Three days later, He rose again,
The devil stood a defeated foe,
Jesus had the keys of hell and death,
He put the devil on show.

Your plan was unfolding, before man's eyes,
You started Your well planned race,
Prophecies about You, all fulfilled,
Everything was falling into place.

When you died upon that splintery cross,
Suffering a death so cruel,
You rose in victory, three days on,
You had won the spiritual duel.

From that day on, Your salvation plan,
Gave a choice, to all on earth,
Reject salvation, and one ends up in hell,
Or accept Your plan of re-birth.

We are called to live a Holy life,
Laying aside our sinful mess,
Living one's life as You have planned,
In truth and faithfulness.

Regardless of what I face in life,
You are ever by my side,
Day or night, good or bad,
From Your presence, I can not hide.

If I go down into the depths,
You are waiting there for me,
If I cross the valley, or climb a mountain,
You deal with me patiently.

You protect me in the fire,
And You calm the raging storm,
Bring peace amid the turmoil,
Ensure I am safe and warm.

You shelter me in winter's cold,
And shield me from Summer's heat,
Make sure I am abundantly blessed,
With something on my feet.

I will always love you, Jesus,
You mean the world to me,
I place my life into Your hands,
In Your presence, I am free.

I thank You Lord for all I am,
And all You created me to be,
You lifted me above the clouds,
And offered salvation to me.

I praise You for such a time as this,
I'm so thankful for my wife,
You are the lover of my soul,
And You are,
THE LOVER OF MY LIFE!

David T. Gilbert.

INTRODUCTION TO 'HOW WILL I BE REMEMBERED?'

This poem is written for those of us who may be a bit concerned about what people would have to say about us after we are gone. But, I suppose a lot of that has to do with the impression we have left on others, and how well known we were when we were once alive. For most of us, we really don't give our attitude, conduct , or example much thought, we seem to have the misconception that nobody is taking notice anyway.

If we chose to live a life for the good of all people that we meet daily, there would be no concern for us after our departure from this earth, because our reputation would speak for us, and our integrity would justify us. As for me, I would like to think that my being here was not wasted on self-interest, but people all over this world who knew me, would recognise that I did my best with what I held in my hands.

So, I present to you some food for thought, so be blessed as you read,

David T. Gilbert.

How will I be remembered?

How will I be remembered,
After the day I would die?
Will I be noted as one living for truth,
A true example for all to live by?

Will people be weeping bitterly,
As they farewell a champion bloke?
Will they thank the Lord of all Creation,
For the good I showed all folk?

What about all those who loved me?
Or so they would quite often say.
Will their comments be kind and favourable,
And be sad that I passed away?

Will they speak of my life in honest truth?
Will their memories be painfully sad?
Will they raise their glasses one more time,
To celebrate the good life that I had?

Will I be remembered as a man of integrity,
And a responsible 'Father Figure?'
Will my children honour the example I was?
In life, was I so much bigger?

And what of my neighbours just next door,
Will they declare me a man of truth?
Will they say of the honest life I lived,
He was surely God's living proof?

We all have concerning questions,
To consider before we die.
We prefer to be remembered for the good,
Letting our sinful past drift by.

But nobody lives a perfect life!
We don't always get it right.
We do our best with what we have,
Life isn't all black and white!

The only answer for this earth,
To escape the oncoming strife,
Is found in Jesus, and Him alone,
He died just to save your life!

The Word of God is an AWESOME book,
The most powerful ever written,
It speaks of God, and the history of man,
Causing multitudes to be smitten.

People from every nation known,
Have been martyred for their faith,
They were too good for our crumbling earth,
They were seeking a much better place!

When people face the Almighty God,
We all will, and that is certain,
For some, it will be a day to rejoice,
For others, it's the final curtain.

We need a Saviour, to intercede,
Who has never yielded to sin.
Jesus truly paid the ultimate price,
Carnal man can't compare to Him.

He shed His Holy, innocent blood,
For the sins of all mankind,
He died to set the captives free,
And open the eyes of the blind.

And when He rose, just three days later,
He rose in complete victory,
He purchased us with His own blood,
Which was the ultimate final plea.

One day we will all face Almighty God,
And be called to give account,
To answer for the lives that we have lived,
Of this, there will be no doubt!

Death seems to be so ever distant,
When we are young and bold,
We have such fun enjoying life,
Without a concern for growing old.

But then, as years go rushing by,
And pain invades your limbs,
You aren't as young as you once were,
So you work out at the Gym.

Then you retire, from all your work,
By then, you're old and grey,
Reminiscing on the past life you had,
And the good times along the way.

You reflect upon past years, and ponder,
Was I the cause of any trouble?
Was I kind and receptive, to all I met?
Did I pray, God bless them double?

We all take life for granted, at times,
Assuming to arise each morn,
Not realising our lives are in His hand,
As we work from dusk till dawn.

As a lifestyle, we should practice well,
To love and do good to all,
God knows what He created us for,
Without Him, we'd surely fall.

So, if you are an optimist,
And believe in a future hope,
Surrender all to the Lord above,
He is you only Living Life rope.

Jesus stands at the door of your heart,
Giving all a precious chance,
To live a Holy life with Him,
It's worth more than just a glance.

No matter how bad your life has been,
There's no sin He won't forgive,
He didn't create you for the fires of hell,
He created you to really LIVE.

When you enter the presence of our God,
He will saturate you with love,
Re-build your life, give you a hope,
Your home will be in Heaven above.

I have served God now, for thirty long years,
I have witnessed many marvellous things,
I am so privileged to know my God,
I love the joy that He brings.

So if you want to really live, with a loving, caring God,
One who will love you as you are,
He is God's Living Word.

Surrender unto Jesus, my Lord,
You will live no greater life,
He will welcome you as a personal friend,
Far from trouble and strife.

ACKNOWLEDGEMENTS

IN MY FIRST book, I mentioned the contribution that certain people had made toward the publishing of my life story, and how much I appreciated their efforts with that contribution, and this second book is possible only due to the dedication of Godly people who lovingly cared enough to see this book make it to the final stage of publication.

People like my Spiritual Father, who is such a humble man and a champion of the faith, I dare not embarrass him by going against his desire to simply serve as a true servant of God.

But I do feel it necessary to thank my Lord and Saviour, Jesus Christ, for His patience and persistence in guiding me to write my book in His way, and for showing me such mercy as I have never known before, and could never hope to know at the hands of any other.

In stating what I have written, there are so many friends and family members that have played a part in the writing of my book, and exercising the most tolerant patience with me, as only friends and family can.

In summary, I will forever be indebted to my wife, BessieMae, for her loving and tolerant attitude toward me at a time when others would have given up in despair, she truly is the love of my life, and I try very hard, daily, to be worthy of her. I can say with total knowledge that "God's grace is truly amazing."

David T. Gilbert.